Original title:
Cookies, Cocoa, and Christmas Cheer

Copyright © 2024 Creative Arts Management OÜ
All rights reserved.

Author: George Mercer
ISBN HARDBACK: 978-9916-90-900-3
ISBN PAPERBACK: 978-9916-90-901-0

## Sharing Secrets of the Season

In the kitchen, flour flies,
And a whisk is spun, oh my!
Baking secrets, silly tricks,
Watch the batter dance and stick.

Sprinkles twinkle, bright and bold,
Chocolate chunks, a treasure trove.
Piping bags, a wild affair,
Some end up in my crazy hair!

From the oven, wafts a dream,
Taste test? Oh, that's a scheme!
One for you and two for me,
Who knew baking could be so free?

As we laugh and share our treats,
Giggles bubble up like sweets.
With each bite, we share a grin,
These moments spark the joy within!

## Warm Embrace in a Dark Cup

In mugs of warmth, the giggles swirl,
A sweet surprise with every twirl.
Marshmallows dance on cream so bright,
As spoon brawls form in frothy fight.

The aroma wraps like a cozy hug,
While the milk mustache's the ultimate snug.
Oh, how we sip with silly glee,
As flavors mix hilariously free!

## Laughter and Spice in the Air

A sprinkle of mischief, a dash of fun,
We mix the spices till we can't wait to run.
Gingerbread men join the wacky race,
With icing smiles and quickened pace.

Baking blunders, a floury fight,
As we slip on dough in candlelight.
Every rise and fall brings hearty laughs,
In our floury joy, we'll take silly drafts!

## Hearths of Cheer on Winter Nights

By the fire where legends are spun,
Warm and cozy, we banter for fun.
Tales of reindeer who prance with flair,
As shadows dance in the laughter we share.

Stockings hung, but who will take a peek?
Maybe a cat, or a friend who's cheeky!
With cocoa spills on the soft white floor,
We giggle softly; oh, we crave more!

## **Playful Sprinkles of Delight**

With little hands, we sprinkle bright,
On treats that vanish in a single bite.
A giggly mess from head to toe,
As flavors pop in the evening glow.

Each crumb that falls brings shouts of glee,
As we race for seconds, just you and me.
In playful chaos, we share our cheer,
Laughter echoing, the season's here!

## Heartfelt Moments in a Sweet Symphony

Gather 'round, the oven's warm,
Flour dusts the floor like a soft charm.
Choco chips and sprinkles fly,
Now watch the dog, oh my, oh my!

With laughter ringing, we taste test,
Burnt edges? Nah, we like them best!
A sprinkle here, a dash of cheer,
Mom's wild kitchen, we hold so dear.

## A Blanket of Flavorful Memories

Whisking throwdowns, laughter spills,
Nose deep in mixing bowls, what thrills!
A sneaky taste here, that loud gasp there,
Who thought that batter could be so rare?

Pudding fights and flour rains,
Sticky fingers, all the gains.
Mom's apron fights more battles too,
As we sculpt sweet shapes that no one knew.

## Dancing Flames and Sweet Cravings

The flames crackle and rise up high,
S'mores on forks make spirits fly.
A gingerbread man takes a wild leap,
While dad pretends to be in a sleep.

With faces painted pure delight,
Somehow we manage to bake all night.
We dance like we're stars on the kitchen floor,
With every bite, we shout for more!

## Nostalgia in Every Warm Sip

In mugs brimming with frothy dreams,
Each sip somehow bursts at the seams.
 Spilling secrets, warming our toes,
  This cozy feel, oh how it grows!

Children giggle, while adults swoon,
A missing ingredient? Just add a tune!
 With every slurp, memories flow,
  Turns out the past was quite the show!

## The Aroma of Joyful Togetherness

Sweet smells waft through the air,
Little hands scatter flour everywhere.
Singing loudly, off-key and bright,
Baking projects turn into a flight.

Laughter erupts, a flour fairy dance,
Mom's secret ingredient? Just take a chance!
The kitchen's a storm, chaos on display,
Whisking up memories that won't fade away.

## Mirth Wrapped in a Ribbon

With ribbons and bows, we wrap up the fun,
Hiding sweet bites, a race has begun.
Mismatched socks, they stick out in style,
As we sneak treats, we giggle a while.

Santa might frown at the crumbs on our shirt,
But joy in our hearts, oh, it can't be hurt!
Unwrapping the glee, with a dash of sprinkles,
Home's full of laughter, where the joy twinkles.

## **Chocoholic's Holiday Delight**

Chocolate rivers run through our dreams,
Overflowing with sweetness, or so it seems.
Spoons dive in deep, oh what a sight,
Who needs a meal when dessert feels just right?

With mischievous smiles, we take our first bite,
Candy-coated giggles dance in the light.
Warnings of sugar? We laugh in reply,
With each chocolaty joy, we reach for the sky!

## A Symphony of Flavors and Festivities

A sprinkle of this and a dash of that,
Creating a mix that makes us all spat.
We dance 'round the table, a culinary show,
As flavors collide, we happily go!

Giggles abound when we taste the surprise,
Flavors mingle boldly, a feast for our eyes.
In this merry kitchen, where spoons truly rule,
We're all chefs of laughter, now that's really cool!

## **Joy Served on a Silver Platter**

Plates piled high with flakes of bliss,
Tiny bites you simply can't miss.
Sprinkles dancing, colors collide,
A temptation hard to hide.

Sweet aromas waft through the air,
Chasing away every ounce of despair.
Giggling faces, laughter so wide,
Serving joy on a friendly ride.

## Candied Memories of the Season

In a jar, memories tightly packed,
Sticky fingers, a taste on the act.
Nostalgic giggles echoing clear,
A sweetness found in holiday cheer.

Spoons dive deep, oh what a sight,
Each scoop's a treasure, pure delight.
As children giggle and grown-ups tease,
It's a rhythm that always aims to please.

## Allure of Spiced Delights

Whispers of cinnamon, a naughty tease,
Baking magic sure to please.
Chop and mix, with grace and glee,
A dance of flavors, just wait and see.

Sprinkled springs and floury dust,
It's a frolic, a joyful thrust.
Laughter spills like melting dough,
A delightful hug, that's how we flow.

## **Euphoria in Every Bite**

Crunchy edges, soft middle bliss,
The taste of mischief, you can't resist.
With every nibble, giggles share,
A burst of happiness fills the air.

Plates are empty, but spirits soar,
Glee found in recipes of yore.
In every morsel, a playful delight,
The season dances, oh what a sight!

## **Sipped Whispers of Togetherness**

In mugs so round, with warmth inside,
Little giggles and secrets collide.
Marshmallows drift like clouds in the night,
Every sip brings pure delight.

Laughter bubbles, sweet scents arise,
While topping the treats, we improvise.
Witty remarks with each little bite,
Together, we craft a cozy delight.

## Flavors of the Festive Season

Spices dance in the air so bright,
With each little taste, our hearts take flight.
Ginger men prance, all dressed in cheer,
Who knew such joy could come from a sphere?

Sprinkles rain down like party confetti,
Each flavor's a friend, and they're all quite petty.
With giggles and splats, we whip and we stir,
Oh, holiday chaos is the very best blur!

## The Elves' Secret Recipe

Little hands mix with glee, oh my,
A dash of this, a pinch of that—oh, why?
They snicker and scheme behind the flour,
Crafting a treat that has all the power.

Rolling in laughter as dough hits the floor,
The elves are a mess, who could ask for more?
The taste of mischief, oh so divine,
Together we'll giggle, and we'll all feel fine.

**Snowflakes on Golden Crust**

Golden discs sparkle, fresh from the heat,
Dancing around in circles, oh, what a treat!
With bites that crunch and flavors that sing,
Who knew such fun could come from one ring?

Twirling and swirling, a sugary dance,
Each little crumb gives us a chance.
To toss and to bite, it's laughter galore,
As we nibble and munch, who could ask for more?

## Celebrations in a Scented Kitchen

In a kitchen stirred with glee,
Flour flies like joyful confetti,
Bowl beats dance to the mixer's tune,
As the clock ticks towards afternoon.

Baking blunders are quite the show,
Frosting splatters, oh what a throw!
Sprinkles rain like confetti bright,
Then taste testers launch a delight.

## **Joyful Crumbs Beneath the Tree**

Beneath the green, the treasures hide,
Crumbly bits are like a guide,
To sugary wonders that make you squeal,
A treat or two are all fair game to steal.

The dog sniffs out a hidden stash,
While kids devour in a hurried crash,
Mom rolls her eyes at the mess they've made,
But giggles follow each delicious raid.

## **A Cozy Flurry of Flavor**

On a winter's night, the oven glows,
With sweet aromas that tickle the nose,
Each bite a wonder, a giggle, a grin,
Between the laughter, new flavors begin.

A sprinkle here, a dash of delight,
Makes every nibble a magical bite,
The madness grows as pans stack high,
Even the cat gives a curious sigh.

## **Threads of Joy in Every Bite**

With every munch, a happy dance,
Flavors twirl, given half a chance,
Each flaky piece a masterpiece,
Spreading silliness, never cease.

Eager hands reach for a steal,
While giggles bubble, it's unreal,
A sprinkle war in the kitchen's whirl,
'Tis the season! Let the flavors unfurl.

## **Embracing the Spirit of Giving**

A jolly old fellow stumbles by,
His pants full of treats, oh my, oh my!
He trips on a cat, falls right in the snow,
With gifts that bounce back, it's quite the show.

The neighbors all gather, what a surprise,
As laughter erupts, the joy multiplies.
Homes decorated bright, with jingle bells clear,
Sharing is caring, spread love and cheer.

## **Flour-Dusted Joys in December**

In the kitchen we dance, with flour on our nose,
Mixing up magic, in bowls it just flows.
The dog licks the beaters with great delight,
While Dad claims he's baking, a true chef tonight.

The timers all buzz, the chaos unfolds,
An army of treats, with stories retold.
We taste-test the batches, with giggles and grins,
And wonder why every dessert comes with sins.

## Vanilla Frosting and Twinkling Lights

The stars twinkle brightly, so do the sprinkles,
As kids make a mess, oh, how laughter crinkles.
Frosting on faces, sweet smudged with glee,
They giggle and yell, 'This is pure jubilee!'

A tree full of bulbs, but has no green,
With sweets hanging low, it's a sugary scene.
The cat climbs the branches to take a quick peek,
A tumble ensues, it's the highlight this week.

## A Hug in a Cup

Warm liquid swirls in a mug held tight,
Like sipping on sunshine, oh what a sight!
A sprinkle of joy, with a dash of delight,
As happy folks gather, it feels just right.

With marshmallows floating like clouds in a dream,
It's cozy as laughter and giggles redeem.
The evening rolls in, with stories to tell,
Each sip is a hug, can you taste it as well?

## A Feast of Light and Laughter

Snowflakes dance and twirl around,
While giggles bounce from ground to ground.
What's that smell? Oh, it's divine,
That treats are waiting right on time.

Grandma's apron, flour-strewn,
Her laughter wild, a merry tune.
Baking blunders all the same,
The dough now looks like a puppy's game.

Frosted faces, cheeky grins,
Who knew the fun would start with sins?
Chasing sprinkles, dodging the cat,
Our winter feast is where it's at!

As we feast with joy and cheer,
Watch out for crumbs, they might appear.
With a wink and smile, we all can share,
A merry time beyond compare.

## Sweet Whispers of Winter Nights

Frosty windows, kisses sweet,
Under blankets, we huddle neat.
Sipping warmth from mugs so wide,
While snowy ghosts outside abide.

Warm laughter mingles with the chill,
As we race for our favorite thrill.
Crafting treats that give a fright,
Who knew that dough could take to flight?

Sprinkles flying, toppings bold,
The dog now wears a crown of gold.
A dash of fun, a pinch of glee,
Who knew baking could be so free?

Jingle bells and cookie trails,
As the laughter fills our sails.
In every bite, a giggle rings,
These winter nights, how joy they bring!

## **The Warmth of Sugar and Spice**

From the kitchen, wafts a tune,
Puppy paws tapping afternoon.
A pinch of joy, a splash of cheer,
Can you believe that it's this time of year?

Silly hats and flour fights,
Marshmallow snowmen, pure delights.
The oven beeps, it's time to play,
With cakes that jiggle in a sneaky way.

Butterflies made of icing bright,
Sneaking tastes when no one's in sight.
With every crumb, we laugh aloud,
In this sweet chaos, we feel so proud.

Happiness served on a platter wide,
Dancing sugar fairies side by side.
What a life, oh can't you see?
Our sweet adventure is all we need!

## **Frosted Dreams by the Fire**

Gather 'round, the glow is warm,
In our cozy nook, there's no alarm.
Logs are crackling, shadows play,
As the tales of mishaps start their sway.

A spoon that flies, oh what a mess,
Pies and pastries, we must confess.
A sprinkle here, a dash of flair,
Our cooking show is quite the affair.

Laughter spills as plates are dropped,
Our hearts are full, our spirits propped.
With every laugh, the hours glide,
What joy it is to bake and bide.

As embers fade and dreams unfold,
In sugar-laden nights, we've bold.
For in this warmth, we find our way,
To frosted dreams that save the day!

**Flavors of the Heart**


In the oven, magic swirls,
The dough's a dance of joy.
A sprinkle here, a pinch of cheer,
It's baking time, oh boy!

A taste of sweetness clings to the air,
While giggles rise like dough.
Flavors swirl like holiday flair,
Who knew flour could steal the show?

Mismatched sprinkles lace each treat,
Some fall like snowflakes down.
Loyal crumbs at every seat,
A crunchy, joyful crown.

As flavors meld, we share the fun,
With bites that dare to sing.
Spiced with love, we all have won,
In laughter, smiles take wing.

## **Frosty Kisses in Every Layer**

Whipped cream clouds float on high,
   Like tiny pillows, they gleam.
A sip warms the heart and the eye,
   A frosty kiss, a sweet dream.

Marshmallows dance like stars above,
   In steaming cups of cheer.
With every sip, it's magic, my love,
   Warming up every ear.

A swirl of chocolate smiles bright,
   Twirling in each cozy mug.
Giggling friends all savor the bite,
   While sharing hugs, oh snug!

As laughter flows and stories blend,
   We sip a festive brew.
With frosty kisses, hearts ascend,
   Creating memories anew.

## Hearthside Blessings

Beside the fire, we gather round,
With treats piled high, oh my!
Each crumb a story, just profound,
As laughter lifts us nigh.

The scent of warmth, a fragrant cloak,
Wrapping us in pure delight.
With every bite, we're all bespoke,
As joy ignites the night.

Crackling logs, a dance of light,
As giggles tumble free.
Our hearthside blessings shine so bright,
In sweet harmony.

Together we share our silly joys,
With stories spun like gold.
Smiles abound with festive noise,
Creating memories bold.

## **Starlit Sips of Delight**

Under the stars, we raise our cups,
With magic swirling inside.
Liquid laughter overflows and erupts,
A joyous little ride.

Each sip, a twinkle in the night,
With flavors that spark and play.
We revel in the merry sight,
As darkness fades away.

Oh, let's stir our hearts with glee,
And sprinkle in a joke.
With every sip, we dance and see,
The laughter we invoke.

With starlit sips, the fun expands,
As friendship fills the air.
Together, we create new plans,
In giggles, we all share.

## **Sweet Delights of Winter's Eve**

In the kitchen, flour flies,
Batter drips and laughter sighs.
Mischief blooms and giggles swell,
Who knew baking could be hell?

Sprinkles rain like festive snow,
The dough won't stop, oh no, oh no!
Burnt edges with a chocolate swirl,
A connoisseur, that clumsy girl!

Frosting's plopped like snowy drifts,
Taste testing leads to crazy shifts.
In a frenzy, they dance and twirl,
Each creation gives a giggly whirl.

Flavors clash, a shocking blend,
Delicious chaos, no end to mend.
But by the time the night is through,
We'll need a nap and a rescue too!

# A Mug Full of Warmth

Boiling water, steam and flair,
A splash of magic, here and there.
With tiny marshmallows, cute and round,
In our mug, warmth can be found.

Sips turn to giggles, spill and splash,
A little chaos, a fun-filled clash.
A dance-off now with sloshy tunes,
Who knew mugs could make such goons?

The cats are loopy, the dog does flip,
There's cocoa on every single lip.
Who needs presents when there's this thrill?
We'll stir up joy with every spill!

At the bottom, secrets lie hidden,
A lump of sweetness has been forbidden.
With mugs in hand, we'll laugh till we sway,
What's in the mug? Who's gonna say?

## **Frosted Whispers of the Season**

Everyone's baking, what a sight,
Doughy struggles into the night.
I try a taste, it's oddly sweet,
Maybe I'll just stick to the treat!

I'll wear an apron, but look out!
Flour cloud and a laughter shout.
Two left feet as I whirl and twirl,
It's only fun when I'll do a whirl.

The oven's on, I check the time,
But someone's pie smells way sublime.
A pop of colors in a swirl of cheer,
With laughter echoing ear to ear.

The final batch is a crispy flop,
But no one's laughing, they can't stop.
So here we stand, with our silly plight,
Creating memories deep into the night!

## Nibbling Under Twinkling Lights

Under bright stars, we gather near,
Nibbles abound, spread out, sincere.
The dog steals a snack without care,
Now holiday cheer fills the air.

Twinkling lights and chatter bright,
Dance around with cookies of night.
Each little bite, a burst of fun,
Oh, the chaos never is done!

Friends are laughing, but I just caved,
In a chocolate trap, I was braved.
Turns out, I've no willpower at all,
I might as well just take the fall.

Sweetness drips from cheeks aglow,
It's a wonderful mess, this we know.
With crumbs on the ground and smiles so wide,
Under twinkling lights, we swallow our pride!

# Confections of Community and Warmth

Gathered 'round the kitchen sink,
Flour fights leave us all in pink.
Sprinkled joy on everything,
Laughter makes the oven sing.

Sloppy hands and giggles loud,
We parade like a flour cloud.
Taste-testing just one more bite,
As ingredients take their flight.

The mixing bowl our stage for flair,
A dance-off with a spoon to share.
The oven's warmth, our cozy fate,
A sweet surprise on every plate.

## The Thrill of Holiday Baking

The timer dings, we shout with glee,
What did we bake? Let's wait and see!
With sugar rushes and silly grins,
Flour snowballs, let the chaos begin!

A sprinkle here, a dash of fun,
Who knew baking could weigh a ton?
Chasing pets, caught in a blur,
Did that dog just steal the stir?

Baking disasters we might recall,
But they just add to our bakeshop's wall.
Embarrassing fails, we take them in stride,
With giggles and hugs on the livelong ride.

**Festive Flavors in the Air**

A whiff of nutmeg, a dash of spice,
In this kitchen, it's a food paradise.
From chocolate drips to butter's craze,
We're all just in a festive daze!

Sticky fingers and melted glee,
What's that drowning in a cup of tea?
A taste adventure, we're lost in bliss,
Did anyone order that chocolate kiss?

Gingerbread houses, a crumbly site,
Who built a tower? It's quite the height!
With frosting rivers and marshmallow peaks,
We cheer for treats and the joy it speaks.

## **A Tapestry of Love and Sweetness**

Baking crafts with a pinch of cheer,
The whisk's a wand when friends are near.
Sticky dough, but hearts are light,
Whipping up joy late into the night.

A dollop here, a bright delight,
Mischievous sprinkles occupy the height.
As joy bubbles over, we dance a jig,
A grand finale with one last dig!

Towers crumble, but spirits soar,
With every treat, we create folklore.
For each sweet bite, a memory to hold,
In every corner, a story unfolds.

## Date with Delight Under the Stars

A sprinkle of flour in the air,
Two bakers dance without a care.
Tasting dough, they giggle loud,
Under the stars, they're feeling proud.

They drop a tray, what a mess!
Sprinkles scatter; oh, the stress!
But laughter erupts, how they jest,
In this sweet chaos, they feel blessed.

## A Biscuit Affair with the Moon


By moonlight glow, they mix and blend,
A doughy love that will not end.
Rolling pins flying all around,
With every laugh, new joy is found.

They sneak a taste, a stolen bite,
Giggles echo through the night.
Flour in hair, they don't care,
In this sweet mess, love is in the air.

## **Melting Hearts and Shared Smiles**

A warm oven hums a tune,
Two friends dance to a cookie groove.
Melted treats and slaps on backs,
Each sugary sight is a joyous act.

Batches burn in their haste to play,
Throw in more sprinkles; who can say?
With every bite, friendship cultivates,
Melting hearts, joy that never waits.

## The Laughter of Yuletide Gatherings

Gather 'round for a tasty game,
Whiskers twitch, all are to blame.
They mix and mash like a merry band,
Each silly comment, a playful hand.

Tasting spoons become a sport,
While sneaky grins ensure rapport.
With each new batch, the joy increases,
In laughter's hold, our heart never ceases.

## Embracing a Sugar-Glazed Night

Sugar sprinkles dance with glee,

Jingle bells sing, oh let it be!

Noses pressed against the glass,

Counting treats, oh what a class!

Frosty windows, laughter plays,

In the kitchen, silly ways.

Whisking joy with every stir,

Flavor fights get quite the blur!

Giggles echo, frosting fights,

Dough is flying, oh what sights!

Behind the counter, grinning wide,

Who knew baking could collide?

**Cocoa Dreams in a Flurry**

Marshmallow clouds on chocolate flies,

Sipping bliss beneath bright skies.

Stirring laughter in a mug,

Hot blends make my heart feel snug.

Raindrops tap against the pane,

Funny faces, never plain.

Twirling spoons in a grand parade,

Sweeter than the finest jade.

Chubby cheeks and crazy hats,

Sipping slowly, chat with cats.

Every sip a joy-filled cheer,

Swirling dreams while we appear.

## Hearthside Laughter and Spice

Crackling fire, storytellers roam,

Cinnamon giggles call us home.

Cookies tossed like snowflakes bright,

A laughter storm, oh what a sight!

Little voices singing loud,

Whirling hugs, a joyous crowd.

Sneaky chefs with plans anew,

Stir it well, then taste the brew.

Pine scents mingle, laughter's near,

Whisking love in every cheer.

Warmth surrounds the silly mess,

Holiday fun, we're truly blessed!

# The Essence of Holiday Comfort

Jolly faces, oh what a sight,

Merry elves take flight tonight.

Sipping warmth with silly straws,

Giggles tumble like snowflakes' claws.

Pudding plops and wobbly cakes,

Mischief brews with all our flakes.

Underneath the twinkling stars,

Baking hopes, we've gone too far.

Frosting fingers, chocolate bliss,

Who knew fun could be like this?

In the chaos, joy is found,

Wrapped in laughter, love abounds!

## **Sweets for the Soul**

Mixing flour with a grin,
Sprinkling joy from within.
Burnt edges add some flair,
Who needs perfect? Who'd care?

Sprinkles dance like tiny stars,
Frosting dreams that heal all scars.
Taste-buds giggle as they play,
Nibble joy, come what may.

Whisking giggles, laughing loud,
A jolly baking, joyful crowd.
Spoonfuls of fun, a dash of jest,
Every bite, a silly quest.

Taste my blunders, take a chance,
Savor sweet goof-ups, let's dance.
With every crumble, we delight,
Merry munching through the night.

## **Celebration Drizzled with Delight**

Chocolate rivers on my shirt,
Oops! That's gonna hurt.
Catch the drips with open mouth,
Sweetness flowing from the south.

Giggling chefs, a flour fight,
Like a scene from pure delight.
Piping bags in clumsy hands,
Frosting lands in funny strands.

Mixing joy with sugar highs,
Baking up our wildest pies.
Laughter swirls like whipped cream's grace,
Flour ghost dances, face-to-face.

In this mess, we find our cheer,
Just a sprinkle, never fear.
With each bite, our hearts take flight,
Jovial chaos feels so right.

## **The Art of Baking Dreams**

Rolling dough with frosted dreams,
Laughter bursts at funny seams.
In the oven, giggles rise,
Sweet aromas, a surprise.

Decorations gone astray,
Who knew sweets could lead to play?
Frosting faces, doughy hands,
Sugar fights in silly bands.

Every whisk a joke in grain,
Baking bliss with laughter's strain.
Taste the chaos, feel the glee,
In this kitchen, let it be.

Oops! The timer's gone off track,
Cakes like slumps, no looking back.
With all the fun, we'll roll along,
In our hearts, we all belong.

## **Gleeful Treats for a Merry Heart**

Choco fudge on the green floor,
Oops! There's puddles by the door.
Bakers laughing, what a sight,
Flour coats in pure delight.

Shortbread figures with goofy grins,
Sugar rush, let's all begin!
Twinkling lights and spilled milk nights,
In our kitchens, fun ignites.

Plates piled high, no one cares,
Bite the funny, share the fares.
Joyful snacks of crazy flair,
Time for treats, beyond compare.

Baking whimsies, fat and bright,
Every nibble feels so right.
In this season of jolly sway,
Laughter leads us on our way.

## Sugar-Plum Wishes and Glee

In the kitchen, a big ol' mess,
Flour flying, oh what a stress!
Mixing joy with a dash of glee,
Licking spoons, just you and me.

Silly smiles, and chocolate streaks,
We're chefs now, or so it speaks,
Tasting sprinkles 'til we turn blue,
Making magic, it's what we do!

Giggles echo, as pans go clang,
The oven's singing its jolly slang,
Frostings fighting for top-tier fame,
Can you guess who'll win the game?

Sugar-plum visions, in frosty air,
Stealing snacks when no one's aware,
Mirthful munching, with a sly little grin,
Wishing this fun would never begin!

## **Crafting Happiness in the Kitchen**

With a whisk in hand, I dance around,
Plopping down dough with a glorious sound,
Sprinkling sugar like magic dust,
In this floury frolic, oh how we trust!

Mixing and mashing, such silly sights,
Batter battles turn into delights,
Why is the counter our favorite stage?
We laugh, we slide, like we're all the rage!

Piping the frosting with utmost flair,
Decorating chaos, without a care,
Hey, whose idea was this wild plan?
Oh wait, was it yours or mine, oh man?

As we clean with a chocolate fight,
Who knew cooking could feel so right?
Bursting with giggles, our hearts overflow,
The love and the mess, it's the best kind of show!

## **Winter's Embrace in Every Nibble**

Frosty nights by the warm, bright flame,
Nibbling on treats, it's part of the game,
Sipping sweet nectar, oh what a thrill,
A cozy wonderland that many will fill!

Snowflakes dance while we munch and chew,
Who knew winter had flavors anew?
Chilly cheeks, but hearts feeling warm,
Our taste buds tangle in a happy swarm!

Giggling together, we take a big bite,
Counting the stars that twinkle at night,
Laughter and crumbs, what a wonderful sight,
In this jolly place that feels just right!

Every nibble brings squeals of delight,
Our playful feast, a whimsical sight,
As songs and joy fill the festive room,
We share in bliss, as laughter goes boom!

## Flavors that Dance in the Cold

Whirling and twirling, flavors galore,
Mixing up magic, oh what a score!
Fruity and nutty, a taste-bud ballet,
We feast on silliness, merry and gay!

Churn up the laughter, sprinkle with cheer,
Wintery wonders are finally here,
Slam dunk the cherries, the pine nuts too,
Our playful banquet, a giddy zoo!

Watch out for sprinkles, they go astray,
A sugary storm in a bright display,
Crafting delights from mornings to night,
With giggles and joy, all feels so right!

Snagging a bite, then running away,
Teasing and giggling, it's our grand play,
With flavors that swirl, we take our stand,
In this frosty wonderland, hand in hand!

## A Toast to Togetherness

Sipping joy in a warm cup,
Spilling laughter, never a flop.
Chubby Santa on the fridge,
Winks at us from the edge.

Belly laughs fill the air,
Funny hats and silly flair.
Jingle bells dance off the wall,
As we pretend to not fall.

Sugar sprinkles, oh so bright,
Mischievous elves in the night.
Fumble, tumble, cookies fly,
Mom's not watching; oh my, oh my!

Raise a glass, we all cheer,
To good times and holiday cheer.
Merry giggles and silly games,
What's this? Who brought the flames?

**Ribboned Packages of Happiness**


Tangled ribbons on the floor,
What a mess, I want some more!
Boxes stacked with a sly grin,
Pull the tape, let chaos begin.

Wrappers flying all around,
Old Aunt Mabel's lost and found.
Giggles echo as we chase,
Each other around this tight space.

Presents peeking, what's inside?
I hope it's not another tie!
The dog steals one and runs fast,
Chasing him, we fall at last.

With each gift comes lots of glee,
What a sight for all to see.
Happy shrieks fill the room,
Gladly dodging impending doom!

## Whimsical Whiffs of Celebration

Fragrant air, a sweet delight,
What's that smell? Oh, what a sight!
Fluffy puffs in the oven sway,
Hoping they won't run away.

Laughter bubbles, oops, too hot,
A cloud of flour, oh what a plot!
Rolling pin? No, that's a sword,
We're the knights of this dessert hoard.

Sprinkling joy with a too firm hand,
A colorful mess is what we planned.
Sweet surprises waiting in line,
The taste test? Should we decline?

Merry mayhem fills the hour,
As we dance with sugar power.
This frolic will never cease,
Until we dive into sweet peace.

## **Moments Baked to Perfection**

An apron tied but still not neat,
Flour fights we won't repeat.
Mixing, stirring with a cheer,
Watch the blender—it's in high gear!

A dash of this, a pinch of that,
Who knew baking could be such a spat?
Muffin tops on the floor abound,
While little ones roll all around.

Silly faces in the glaze,
As we work in merry haze.
Tiny hands reach for a taste,
Quick! Grab the plates, don't let them waste!

Voices echo, joy aglow,
In this kitchen, love will flow.
For in every laugh, every mix,
Is a recipe for our happy fix.

## Whimsical Wonders Beneath the Stars

Under the sky, a sweet delight,
Baked goods rise, a charming sight.
Laughter rings through the frosty air,
Giggling friends in hats to wear.

Sprinkling sugar in a flurry,
Each bite taken, no need to hurry.
Flavors dance like twinkling lights,
Crumbs ignite our silly fights.

Chasing crumbs, oh what a game,
Frosting fights will spark the fame.
With every bite, we squeal and cheer,
Under the twinkling light, we steer.

Jolly faces, giggles burst,
Sweet creations are our first.
In this night, with joy we sing,
Let's see what the oven will bring!

## A Calendar of Delectable Joys

Each day unveils a treat so grand,
Nibbling sweets from all around.
The calendar smiles, full of cheer,
With a sticky fingered volunteer.

One day fruit, the next a swirl,
Making mischief, we laugh and twirl.
Is it magic or just our knack?
Every morsel brings the laughter back.

Whisking dreams in a bowl so wide,
A dash of giggles, a sprinkle of pride.
With powdered sugar on our face,
This festive fun, a cozy place.

Baking blunders make us roar,
Frosting fights—who could ask for more?
In this month of sweet cat-tails,
Wrapped in joy, we'll tell our tales!

## Hearth-side Serenades of Delight

The fire crackles, warmth sets in,
Silly songs and teasing grins.
Melted chocolate stains the floor,
What's a kitchen for but fun galore?

We gather 'round with glee and cheer,
While the oven hums, we all draw near.
A pop of zest ignites the night,
With dancing sparks, we feel just right.

Our lamps glow gold, stories shared,
With tasty bites, we are well-prepared.
Under the mistletoe we sneak,
Not just for kisses—sweetness we seek!

From gooey goods to floured feet,
Each laugh unfolds, a special treat.
It's a cozy time, full of charm,
As visions of sweetness keep us warm.

**Treasuring Tasteful Moments**

We gather 'round for a merry spree,
Whisking laughter, oh what glee!
In flour clouds, our spirits soar,
With every taste, who could want more?

Mixing flavors, playful and bright,
Creamy blobs take playful flight.
With every mishap, we just can't stop,
Baked goodness rises, we dance and hop.

The playful banter fills the air,
As we lunge for treats with joyful flair.
Chocolate drips and sprinkles fall,
Our radiant smiles say it all.

Sweet surprises in every bite,
Our hands are messy, our hearts so light.
In this tasty fest, we find our song,
These moments shared are never wrong!

## Mirth and Magic on the Menu


In the kitchen, chaos brews,
Flour flies like confetti hues.
Taste testers dive into the mix,
Sprinkling giggles, sharing laughs and tricks.

Spoons dance like they're in a race,
Each flavor fights for precious space.
Baking powder does a jig,
As laughter erupts, we all feel big.

Choco chips jump in surprise,
When a dough ball meets the skies.
A floured cat joins in the cheer,
Paws covered, oh dear, oh dear!

At last, they cool, all golden brown,
Confectionery crowns for all the town.
With every bite, a fantasy spun,
In merry madness, we've all just begun!

**Frosty Nights with Sweet Companions**

Winter's chill is in the air,
With bundled folks, we find our flair.
A mug's held high with frothy dreams,
As snowflakes ride on cocoa streams.

The carolers sing, their voices bright,
While friends toss snowballs with pure delight.
A gingerbread man wobbles past,
"Catch me if you can!"—a sweet, bold blast.

Marshmallow hats adorn our heads,
While peppermint stirs the candy threads.
Giggles erupt with every spills,
Outraged hot chocolate, as laughter fills.

Under twinkling lights, we bask,
With frosty drinks and festive tasks.
Laughter flies like starlit sparks,
Creating wonders, leaving marks!

## **Glazed Delights of the Season**

In the oven, a warm surprise,
Baking goods make us all wise.
Sprinkled sugar, a shimmery sight,
Ready for munching by festive light.

The clock ticks down, the tension soars,
Shiny treats behind kitchen doors.
A snickerdoodle slips, takes a leap,
While all of us vow not to peep.

Frosting swirls in a glorious mess,
Tasting 'oops' adds to the stress.
"Less is more!" a friend once said,
As we practically eat the spread.

Bite by bite, we gleefully share,
Amid chuckles, we breathe the air.
Glazed wonders melt with every cheer,
In the sweetest of gatherings, joy is near!

## Sprinkled with Laughter and Love

Gather 'round for surprises sweet,
As we master the art of the treat.
Roll and pat with giggles abound,
In whimsical bliss, our joy is found.

Each shape we make, a cartoon fate,
Fumbling hands that can hardly wait.
One cookie shapes like a goofy dog,
As everyone snorts and starts to clog.

Melted morsels more than intended,
"Looks like we've blended!" we all contended.
With frosting stars and sprinkles bright,
Our culinary craft's sheer delight!

As the evening dims, the laughter stays,
With scrumptious treats to fill our days.
In every bite, magic unfolds,
Lavished in warmth, our hearts are gold!

## Magic in Each Sprinkle

In the kitchen, flour flies,
Baking chaos in disguise.
A pinch of mischief in the bowl,
Laughter rising, that's the goal.

Chocolate smudges on my face,
The dog is now in a race.
Rolling dough with every spin,
Who knew fun could taste like sin?

A sprinkle here, a sprinkle there,
Tip-toeing without a care.
The timer dings, a tasty sound,
Sweet creation all around.

My apron's stained, I can't deny,
Yet smiles bloom, oh me oh my!
With every bite, a giggle spills,
Sweet surprises, endless thrills.

## Melodies of Marzipan and Merriment

Notes of sweet, yodeling dough,
Singing loudly, high and low.
The bowl is dancing, whisk in hand,
A rhythm born from sugar land.

Frosting fights and cherry wars,
I've lost my battle in the scores.
A cupcake tower won't hold still,
While sprinkles rain like candy thrill.

Piped-out joy from tips gone wrong,
Who knew pastry could be strong?
Fondant figures start to sway,
As giggles lead the happy way.

Marzipan reindeer, oh so bright,
Sashay into the festive night.
Mixing laughter, love, and cheer,
A melody of joy draws near.

## The Gift of Sweet Remembrance


Wrapped in foil and ribbon tight,
Each little treat brings pure delight.
A nibble here, a morsel there,
Oh, who remembers calories? Fair!

Grandma's recipe, a family lore,
The secret's spilled — I need some more!
A taste of home in each small bite,
With every flavor, spirits ignite.

Milk mustaches look so fine,
While cookie crumbs make stars align.
As children giggle, grown-ups sneeze,
Sugar magic brings us to our knees.

In every package, memories shine,
Sweet nostalgia wrapped in twine.
With a wink, we share a toast,
To treats that make us laugh the most.

## **Hearthside Hues of Delight**

Gathered 'round the warming fire,
Sipping dreams, our hearts aspire.
Sweet scents waft through chilly air,
Wrapped in laughter, warmth, and care.

A marshmallow battle sparks anew,
Fluffy pebbles in a gooey stew.
Hilarity reigns in this warm place,
With faces smeared in a sugary race.

Fireside tales of silly fails,
As festive fun fills all the trails.
Singing songs both flat and bright,
Our goofy spirits take to flight.

As the night wraps all in glee,
Each little mess, pure jubilee.
In every giggle, we find our way,
To hearts embraced this joyful day.

## **Melted Wishes Beneath the Stars**

In a kitchen, oh so bright,
Frosting flies like a silly kite.
Sprinkles dance like stars at night,
Sugar high, what a funny sight!

Flour clouds cover our heads,
Laughter bursts, ignore the threads.
Mixing bowls, they spin and spread,
While mom trips and laughs instead!

Chocolate drips from every spoon,
Caught red-handed, oh what a boon!
The pantry's now a wild typhoon,
We'll clean it up—maybe by June!

For under stars, with pure delight,
We bake our dreams till they take flight.
With giggles echoing in the night,
Melted wishes, oh what a sight!

## Baked Treasures of Enchantment

In the oven, treasures dull,
Baking magic, hear the hull.
Towers of dough rise, almost full,
Mom's cookies—bless this culinary pull!

Flavors hidden, a secret hunt,
Chasing crumbs, we're on the front.
Fortune's cookie says to stunt,
A bite too late, our bellies grunt!

Whisking dreams with giggly flair,
Spills and thrills, we take the dare.
Unique shapes we create with care,
But somehow they become a bear!

At the table, jam jars clash,
We spread and snack, oh what a bash!
Laughter rises with every smash,
Baked treasures never go out with a crash!

## **Sipping Joy on Frosted Mornings**

Frosty glass and comfy chairs,
Stirring pots—who really cares?
Slurping sounds, we make a pair,
Laughter floats in crisp cold air.

Marshmallow fluff takes flight in glee,
On heads, it lands; oh look at me!
Sipping joy, oh can't you see?
We're like kids, wild and free!

Mugs in hand, stories unfold,
Hot delights that never get old.
In every cup, a tale retold,
We sip and giggle, life's pure gold!

As icy winds swirl outside,
We snuggle in, no need to hide.
With every laugh, our hearts abide,
Sipping joy, forever tied!

## **Whirls of Cinnamon and Grace**

In the air, a spicy twist,
Like a chef, we can't resist.
Rolling dough with a wink and twist,
Creating shapes we can't assist!

'Tis a dance, in twirls we bake,
Flour on noses, what a mistake!
Giggles burst with every shake,
In this kitchen, merry we make!

Pies abound, with crusts that gleam,
Lifting spirits like a dream.
We share our laughs, a silly team,
In every bite, a cinnamon theme!

As the oven warms our hearts,
With frosted joy, the fun imparts.
In whirls of love, the laughter starts,
Together we are the finest arts!

## Morsels of Magic Beneath the Tree

Under the tree, a sneaky snack,
A little elf left crumbs in a pack.
With sprinkles and laughter, they dance in delight,
As chaos erupts on this festive night.

The dog in the corner, he sniffs and he dreams,
Of chocolate adventures and sweet, gooey schemes.
While children gamble with crumbs on the floor,
Whispering wishes, they all want more!

A bite here and there, it's all in good fun,
With giggles and mess, oh what's done is done!
The magic of flavors, a delightful charade,
As crumbs tell the stories of joy they've made.

As the clock strikes twelve, the chaos subsides,
With satisfied grins and contented sighs.
In this jolly moment, all cares disappear,
For who needs perfection when joy's full of cheer?

## The Kindness of a Home-Baked Heart

A bowl of mischief, some sugar and spice,
Flour clouds swirling, oh isn't this nice?
Whisking up laughter with a pinch of surprise,
As spatulas dance, oh how time flies!

An apron disaster, a gooey romance,
With each little spill, we all take a chance.
A sprinkle of giggles, a dash of delight,
As we bake up some smiles on this frosty night.

What's baking up there? Is that laughter I hear?
Or just the sound of a maybe burnt sphere?
With a taste test fiasco, we all take a bite,
And declare everything's "just perfect" tonight!

So gather 'round friends, with a grin oh so wide,
As we munch and we crunch, with our hearts open wide.
For kindness emerges in layers so sweet,
In this home-baked magic, we find joy to eat.

## Chocolate Fables and Cheerful Tales

In an oven of fun, where stories unfold,
There dwell tales of brownies, both daring and bold.
With each little scoop, a fable is spun,
Of dragons and fudge, oh, this baking is fun!

A sprinkle of silly, a dash of surprise,
With smiles that twinkle and laughter that flies.
When the dough starts to wink and the cake gives a cheer,

We all sit and marvel at what has appeared.

With frosting so creamy, it's hard to resist,
We nibble and giggle, oh how can we miss?
Each bite leads to laughter, each flavor a plot,
In this chocolate adventure, we're all pretty hot!

So gather your stories, your tales near and far,
Let's bake and create our own sweet memoir.
For joy is the magic in all that we bake,
With chocolatey wonders, we make no mistake!

## Gathering Around the Hearth

Come one, come all, to the hearth's gentle glow,
Where laughter and sweetness begin to overflow.
With mugs overflowing and smiles on our face,
  We all share the warmth of this joyful space.

A plate piled high with delights we create,
Here's hoping the calories can wait until late!
The dog wants a nibble, the cat claims the chair,
  In this merry chaos, there's magic to share.

As tales come alive in the flickering light,
With giggles and hiccups, the mood feels so right.
We raise our mugs high, for toast after toast,
  To the fun and the giggles, we love the most!

So gather your friends, let the stories appear,
In this circle of warmth, we've plenty of cheer.
For nothing can beat the warmth that we find,
  In the spirit of sharing, and leaving woes behind.

## **A Canvas of Flavor and Joy**

In the kitchen, chaos reigns with glee,
Flour on my nose, what a sight to see!
Mixing up magic with a spoon in hand,
A scoop of laughter, oh isn't it grand?

Batter splatters like rain in a storm,
Stirring up giggles is the ultimate norm.
Sprinkles like confetti all over the floor,
Each tablespoon stolen, I just want more!

Gingerbread men dance, sturdy and stout,
With icing on their belts, no hint of doubt.
They'll save some for Santa, or so they say,
But I'll sneak a few pieces, I must admit, hey!

As the timer dings with a glorious sound,
A mix of sweet chaos, our joy knows no bound.
From doughy delight to golden brown cheer,
In this laughing kitchen, all flavors are dear!

## **Glowing Hearts and Delicious Scents**

Whipped cream clouds float high in the air,
Chocolate drips down, oh what a flair!
The snowflakes outside paint a picture so bright,
While inside we feast in our cozy delight.

Marshmallows frolic in mugs piled high,
Giggles erupt with each frothy sigh.
The cat's on the counter, eyeing the fun,
As we sip on sweetness till the day is done.

Christmas lights twinkle, a sparkling show,
Yet nothing compares to the joy we sow.
A pinch of silliness, a dash of surprise,
Bringing laughter together with wide-open eyes.

The aroma swirls like a festive parade,
Whispers of sweetness, a flavorful charade.
With family beside, in this cheerful affair,
We revel in moments no one can compare!

## Harmony in Every Flavorful Layer

In the pantry, secrets all lined up in rows,
Frosting and sprinkles in a flurry of shows.
Mixing mishaps, oh dear, what a sight!
But laughter fills the air, making everything right.

Pies stacked high and laughter even more,
With spoons as our weapons, we're ready for war!
Each bite a giggle, a delightful surprise,
As flavors collide, we can't disguise!

The oven hums tunes of sweet old delight,
As we dance in our aprons, a humorous sight.
Who knew baking could lead to such fun?
As we taste each layer, there's room for everyone!

Every mishap leads to a tale to tell,
With flour on faces, we know it too well.
In this whimsical world, we gather with cheer,
Making memories sweeter, each holiday year!

## Enchanted Evenings of Taste

The moon spills its light on a table set wide,
As treats glimmer softly, we sit side by side.
With puffs of delight and a sprinkle of fun,
Our laughter flows freely, a feast just begun.

Napkins are tossed as we dive into bliss,
Each bite a giggle, a flavor-filled kiss.
The cat claims a cookie, with a mischievous glance,
While we share our secrets in a sugary dance.

Great-auntie's fruitcake, a legendary tale,
With tales incoherent but never too stale.
We cheer for her courage as we take a bite,
And savor that moment, cozy and bright.

With starlit horizons and hearts full of cheer,
Each flavor a memory, our evening sincere.
Enchanted by laughter, in flavors we dwell,
These magical moments, we cherish so well!

## **Journeys Flavored with Love**

In the oven, a sweet aroma swirls,
Like a hug in a jar, it twirls.
Sprinkle some laughter, add a grin,
Baking up memories, let the fun begin.

Roll the dough like life's silly dance,
With flour on noses, we take a chance.
Chasing crumbs like a hungry hound,
In this merry mess, joy is found.

Stirring up giggles with a wooden spoon,
While chocolate chips laugh, making us swoon.
A pinch of chaos, a dollop of cheer,
The best kind of gathering, far and near.

From famished nibblers to mischievous gnomes,
Sweets on our lips, and sparkle in homes.
In the kitchen, all worries take flight,
With each tasty morsel, oh what a delight!

## **Tantalizing Traditions that Bind**

Gather 'round the table, set it up right,
With smudges of chocolate, oh what a sight!
Recipes passed down, secrets they share,
Laughter and crumbs fill up the air.

Grandma's old apron, a treasure of stains,
Whisking up joy, as everyone gains.
The dog's on the lookout, hoping for scraps,
While we're all grinning, with giggles and raps.

The great sugar rush is a whirl of delight,
With wobbly frosting, that just isn't right.
Decorated with love, and a sprinkle of fun,
In this tasty tradition, we're all number one!

Cheers of delight, as we nibble and munch,
We trade little stories, one silly bunch.
With each laugh and snack, our hearts will entwine,
Celebrating moments, oh how they shine!

# A Touch of Nostalgia in Every Bite

Baking takes me back to times gone by,
With giggles of children and flour-filled sky.
Under the mistletoe, that twinkling display,
Every bite whispers of a magical day.

The rolling pins dance, like a merry parade,
With laughter and sprinkles, we happily invade.
A dash of awkward, a heap of delight,
In this kitchen of chaos, all feels just right.

From bites that crunch to those that goo,
Each flavor a memory, dipped in the brew.
A nibble of laughter, a slice of the past,
In the warmth of these moments, our hearts hold fast.

So chew on this tale, let joy be your guide,
With a wink and a nod, and hearts open wide.
In each tasty morsel, together, we unite,
A combo of memories that feels just right!

# **Chorus of Holiday Indulgence**

Singing in the kitchen, a joyful refrain,
Whisking up mischief, oh what a gain!
Batches of laughter, just warming our hearts,
Making sweet magic, that's where it starts.

Frosting on noses, and giggles that soar,
As the culinary chaos begins to pour.
Sprinkles raining down like confetti of fun,
With every wild bite, we're all the same one.

Oh come gather 'round, let's savor this cheer,
In our merry little realm, everyone's dear.
With forks at the ready, and spirits all bright,
We'll indulge together, into the night!

So lift up your glasses, to laughter we raise,
During this season, let's set hearts ablaze.
In the symphony of flavors, we dance and we play,
With laughter as our music, let's seize the day!

Milton Keynes UK
Ingram Content Group UK Ltd.
UKHW020044271124
451585UK00012B/1047